God's World of Weather

written by HENO HEAD, JR.
illustrated by RUSTY FLETCHER

for Mom and Dad

© 2000 by Standard Publishing, a division of Standex International Corporation, Cincinnati, Ohio.
All rights reserved. Bean Sprouts™ and the Bean Sprouts design logo are trademarks of Standard Publishing.
Printed in the United States of America. Cover design by Robert Glover.

07 06 05 04 03 02 01 00   5 4 3 2 1

Library of Congress Card Number: 99-66967
ISBN 0-7847-1101-1

Standard
Publishing
Cincinnati, Ohio

In the first book of the Bible, Genesis, we read that God made many things. He made the sun, the moon, the planets, and the stars. He also made the earth, the sky, and the ocean. And God saw that everything he made was good.

God made all these things to work together in special ways. The sun, air, and water work together to make WEATHER.

Weather is what's happening in the air outside each day. God brings us all kinds of weather—sunny days, rainy days, and even perfect-for-sledding snowy days.

Let's take a closer look at the three parts of our weather: sun, air, and water. More sunlight hits the middle of the earth, the EQUATOR, than anywhere else. Weather at the equator is hot.

The top and bottom of the earth are called the POLES. The poles don't get much direct sunlight. For that reason, weather at the poles is very cold.

The heat or cold of the air that we feel is called the TEMPERATURE. Temperature can be measured by using a THERMOMETER. Look at these two thermometers. Which place is cool? Which place is warm? What's your favorite temperature?

Places near the equator are hot all year round. The poles are cold all year round. But places in between the equator and the poles have weather that changes all year round. Why do you think that is?

The weather changes as the earth moves around the sun at a tilt. Look at the picture. When a part of the earth is tilted toward the sun, that part will be warmer. When a part is tilted away, that part will be cooler. Based on these changes, we divide the year up into four SEASONS of weather: winter, spring, summer, and fall.

Now let's take a closer look at our air. Do you see anything? Nope? That's because our air is a see-through blanket of gases that covers the earth.

As sunlight heats the air, the air begins to move and swirl across the earth. Do you know what we call this moving air? That's right, it's WIND! We can't see wind, but we can see what the wind moves.

Winds are named for the direction they come from. The four main directions on earth are north (N), south (S), east (E), and west (W). Wow, it's a windy day! What direction is today's wind coming from?

Winds can be slow and gentle or fast and powerful. When cool air meets warm air, the winds that develop can create a dangerous, fast-moving column of air. This circling wind is called a TORNADO.

HURRICANES can also be very destructive. A hurricane begins over the ocean, gaining energy from heat and the whirling winds of a storm.

It's important to pay attention to the weather whenever bad storms are in your area so you know what to do. If you ever see a big storm coming, make sure to listen to your parents and get to a safe place as fast as you can! And remember, God is even more powerful than the most powerful wind on earth!

How do big storms start? Well, look at what we know about water and find out!

The way that water moves from the earth to the air and back to the earth is called the WATER CYCLE. God did a great thing when he created the water cycle.

Every time it rains, you can see the water cycle in action. The sun warms water on the earth's surface. Some of the water gets so hot that it turns into WATER VAPOR, a gas. The vapor collects in the air as CLOUDS. When the air can hold no more water in the clouds, the water falls back to the earth in the form of rain or snow.

Remember that cloud you just saw on the last page? Not all clouds look like that one. There are lots of different kinds of clouds.

Thin, wispy CIRRUS clouds occur high in the sky and often mean rain is coming. Flat STRATUS clouds hang low in the sky and make dull, gray days. White and fluffy CUMULUS clouds appear often on nice sunny days.

Sometimes they seem to form pictures in the sky. Do you see any pictures in these cumulus clouds?

Clouds with dark bottoms bring rain. They look dark because there is so much water in them that the sun can't shine through the thick cloud. However, if the sun shines through raindrops, do you know what we will see? A RAINBOW! The colors of rainbows are always in the same order. What colors do you see?

Sometimes clouds are so low that they touch the ground. We call these clouds FOG. Have you ever been in fog? It's hard to see where everything is, isn't it? Hey, where are you?

The biggest clouds are called CUMULONIMBUS. These clouds may be over eight miles tall. They bring thunderstorms, with thunder and lightning.

LIGHTNING is a giant spark of static electricity. Have you ever walked across the carpet and then touched a doorknob? Did you get a little shock? That was static electricity, the same kind of electricity that makes lightning.

A bolt of lightning is hot. It heats the air. The hot air moves away from the lightning very fast and makes a rumbling sound. We call this THUNDER. It's always best to go indoors when a thunderstorm comes.

If the temperature of the air is warm when the clouds are heavy with water, the water comes down to the earth as rain. But what happens when the temperature is cold?

If the air is cold, we may get SLEET or SNOW. Sleet is frozen rain. SNOWFLAKES are made from water vapor that freezes. God makes each snowflake different and special—just like he made me and you!

Now that we know so much about God's weather, let's read this weather map together! I always wanted to be a TV weatherman! Can you tell what God is doing with the weather today?

God saw that everything he made was good,
including all kinds of weather. And we can see that, too!
Thank you, God!